W9-AXR-848

THANKSGIVING DAY

A Crowell Holiday Book

THANKSGIVING DAY

By ROBERT MERRILL BARTLETT

Illustrations by W. T. MARS

Chapter II -1988-1989

THOMAS Y. CROWELL COMPANY · NEW YORK

FOR SARAH ELIZABETH

75 18

CROWELL HOLIDAY BOOKS

Edited by Susan Bartlett Weber

New Year's Day
Lincoln's Birthday
St. Valentine's Day
Washington's Birthday
Purim
St. Patrick's Day
Passover
Easter
Arbor Day
May Day
Mother's Day
Flag Day
The Fourth of July

Labor Day
The Jewish New Year
Columbus Day
United Nations Day
Halloween
Election Day
Thanksgiving Day
Human Rights Day
Hanukkah
Christmas
The Jewish Sabbath
Indian Festivals
Skip Around the Year

People have always given thanks at
harvest time. They are glad to have
food for the winter and celebrate with
feasting and prayers of thanksgiving.

Long ago the people of Greece had a
harvest festival. It was in the fall after
the grain was cut. Ripe apples, pears,
and plums hung on the trees.

Heralds traveled from village to village. They blew their trumpets and called everyone to the celebration.

The people visited shrines of Demeter, the goddess of the harvest. They carried gifts of grain to lay before her.

The Romans, too, gave thanks at the harvest season. Their goddess was Ceres. They believed Ceres guarded their crops and made them grow well. They honored her with parades, dancing, sports, and feasting.

Another ancient thanksgiving was the Feast of Booths. It was celebrated by the Jews in the land of Canaan. They built little booths from branches and leaves. In them they put fruits and vegetables from the fields. Then they gave thanks to God for their crops.

Later the Christians in Europe said prayers to bless the planting and the reaping of the harvest. They believed that God watched over the seeds in the earth.

At harvest time the farmers decorated themselves with ribbons and flowers. They sang as they walked home beside their wagons full of grain.

The Pilgrims started the American thanksgiving. They came to Plymouth, Massachusetts, in 1620. They were English citizens who demanded the right to read the Bible and worship God as they chose. They also demanded freedom from unfair laws.

Queen Elizabeth I and King James I of England were very cruel to the Pilgrims. They put many of them in prison and killed many of their leaders.

Some Pilgrims fled to Holland where the kind Dutch people helped them. They lived there twelve years. But they wanted a country of their own. So they planned to sail to America.

John Robinson, a teacher from Cambridge University, was the Pilgrim

leader and minister. But he was not able to go to America.

So William Brewster was chosen to take his place. He was not a minister, but he was wise and good.

William Bradford also helped the Pilgrims. Later they elected him governor of their colony thirty-one times. He wrote a famous book about the Pilgrims, called *Of Plimoth Plantation*. It can be seen today in the Statehouse in Boston, Massachusetts.

One hundred and two passengers
came on the little ship, the *Mayflower*.
They cooked, ate, and slept all crowded
together. They were often very seasick.

Day after day they ate salt fish, salt pork, and hard biscuits. Now and then there was oatmeal with molasses, and a bit of cheese.

There were thirty-four children on the ship. Then a baby was born during the voyage. He was named Oceanus Hopkins.

The children played cat's cradle and blindman's buff. Maybe they listened to sea stories told by Captain Christopher Jones.

It was a stormy voyage lasting sixty-six days. Everyone was glad when the *Mayflower* reached Cape Cod on November 21.

For several weeks the men explored Cape Cod. Then they sailed across Massachusetts Bay to Plymouth. There they found a safe harbor and springs of fresh water.

The men rowed ashore in their shallop. They had to cut down trees and start building houses right away. The country was covered with oak, chestnut, hickory, and pine.

No Indians lived in Plymouth then. A sickness had killed many of them and the rest had moved away. The Pilgrims found a few patches of cleared ground and some corn buried in baskets.

That winter the Pilgrims had very little food to eat. They were always hungry and cold. Nearly all of them were sick, and one half of them died.

The people who were left felt braver when spring came. They planted wheat, barley, and peas. They had brought the seeds with them from England.

One day two friendly Indians arrived. They were Samoset and Squanto.

Later Squanto brought Chief Massasoit to visit. The Pilgrims welcomed the big chief of the Wampanoags. They made a treaty of peace with him. For fifty-five years there was no fighting between the Pilgrims and the Indians.

The Indians gave the Pilgrims corn, beans, and squash to plant. Squanto taught them to put three herring in each hill of corn to make the soil richer. They stood guard with their muskets to keep the crows from eating the seeds and the wolves from digging up the herring.

Squanto showed them how to catch the herring in the brook. He showed them how to catch eels, fish, and lobsters, and where to dig clams.

The Pilgrims watched eagerly as the first green blades peeked through the soil. They worked hard all summer in the fields. They knew their lives depended on this harvest.

In the fall they gathered the crops. The wheat and barley had grown well. The corn had grown best of all.

By harvest time seven houses were finished. They had clapboard sides and

windows covered with oiled paper. The roofs were made of thatched reeds. The children climbed a ladder into the loft where they slept.

The Pilgrims were happy as they stored away their harvest. So they decided to celebrate. In October, 1621, they held their first thanksgiving.

They invited the Indians to join them. Ninety braves came with their chief, Massasoit.

Everyone had to help prepare the feast. The older girls, Desire Minter, Priscilla Mullins, and Elizabeth Tilley, turned the spits and stirred the kettles of chowder. Mary Chilton and Remember Allerton looked after the youngest children. The Brewster boys, Love and Wrestling, helped the men keep the fires burning.

The Indians liked the children and tried to play with them. They also explored the strange cottages. Their own houses were round and made of bark.

The Indians brought five deer which
they had shot with bows and arrows.
The Pilgrims had shot wild turkeys
with their matchlock muskets. There
were corn meal cakes and biscuits of
coarse wheat flour. There was roasted

corn. There were salads of watercress and leeks. And dried plums, cherries, and gooseberries.

The food was cooked in fireplaces and over open fires. The spits sizzled with venison, turkey, geese, and ducks. Lobsters boiled in big iron pots. Oysters and clams roasted in the coals.

At last the feast was ready. The Pilgrims and Indians ate with their fingers or with clam shells. Their plates were made of wood or pewter. They drank red and white wine made from wild grapes. It was a gay and noisy party.

The Pilgrims wore bright clothes of Lincoln green, red, blue, purple, and russet brown. The Indians wore aprons of deer leather. They had skins of fox, bear, or moose about their shoulders. Some had feathers in their well-greased hair. Their faces were painted with red and white lines.

After the feasting they played games and had contests. There were foot races, Indian wrestling, and pitching the bar.

The Indians shot with their bows and arrows. The Pilgrims drilled and marched with their armor. They fired their matchlocks.

After three days the Indians went home. Soon two more ships came with settlers. There was not enough food to go around.

Everyone was hungry once again. More wild game and fish were hard to find. The women and children looked on the beaches for clams and in the woods for nuts.

But the Pilgrims kept working. They
sawed logs and cut clapboards. They
traded with the Indians for beaver and
otter furs. They picked sassafras. These
things were sent to England to pay for
the *Mayflower* voyage.

The first shipload of clapboards and furs was captured by pirates. So was the second shipload. The Pilgrims had to start all over again. But they had great courage.

In the spring of 1623 the Pilgrim leaders gave each person an acre of land. At first they had shared the land. Now each family planted its own fields. All set to work with new spirit.

For many weeks there was no rain. The Pilgrims were afraid there would be no harvest. So Governor Bradford called for a day of prayer to God. The people met in the fort-meetinghouse on the hill above the village.

For eight hours they prayed for rain. Some of the children fell asleep and a deaconess tickled their noses with a turkey feather. Many Indians came, too. They prayed to the Great Spirit to send rain.

When they left the fort-meeting-house the sky was gray. Clouds gathered and soon a soft rain began to fall. It rained off and on for fourteen days. The corn grew green again and the hearts of the Pilgrims were glad.

Two more things made the Pilgrims happy. The ship *Anne* sailed into Plymouth harbor. It brought some of the families left behind in Holland and England.

And the village was almost finished. Nineteen houses and three common houses lined the street.

So the Pilgrims decided to have another thanksgiving. Governor Bradford made it a day for giving "glory, honor, and praise with thankfulness to our good God."

On the second thanksgiving morning the Pilgrims put on their best clothes. They marched to the fort-meetinghouse. There they gave thanks to God for all their blessings.

As the years passed, many other colonists settled in America. They, too, had thanksgivings at special times.

In 1783, George Washington, the first President of the United States, proclaimed the first thanksgiving day for all Americans. The people gave thanks for their freedom from England.

Not until 1863 did Thanksgiving become a national holiday. Then President Abraham Lincoln made the last Thursday of November Thanksgiving Day.

Today Thanksgiving is a happy time when families gather together. Like the Pilgrims, they dress in their best clothes and go to church. They sing harvest hymns and pray. Then they hurry home for the feast.

Grandparents, parents, brothers and sisters, uncles, aunts, cousins, and friends meet around the long dinner table. The huge roasted turkey is carved. Then come dressing and gravy,

scalloped oysters, potatoes, squash,
turnips, onions, cranberry sauce, pickles,
and jelly. Last of all are the pumpkin
and mince pies.

They eat and eat. And talk and talk.
They are almost as noisy as the Pilgrims

and Indians at the first Thanksgiving.

Sometimes a little boy falls asleep at the table. But no one tickles his nose with a feather to wake him up. Instead his grandfather takes him in his arms and carries him off to bed.

ABOUT THE AUTHOR

Thanksgiving is an especially appropriate subject for Robert Merrill Bartlett, for he was for many years the minister of one of New England's famous colonial churches. He is now an active member of Plimouth Plantation (which is restoring the original Pilgrim Village) and lectures to clubs, schools, churches, and civic groups about that organization's plans.

Born in Indiana, Dr. Bartlett was graduated from Oberlin College and Yale School of Divinity. He has taught in universities in this country and in Peiping, China. Dr. Bartlett's books for young people include *They Stand Invincible: Men Who Are Reshaping Our World* and *With One Voice: Prayers from Around the World.*

ABOUT THE ARTIST

At the age of nine, W. T. Mars provided the illustrations for a children's book written by his mother, a well-known author. After attending the lycée in his native city of Cracow, Poland, Mr. Mars pursued his interest in art at the Academy of Fine Arts in Cracow and Warsaw, and later in France and Italy.

Mr. Mars's paintings have been purchased by museums in Sweden, England, and Scotland, and several are included in Polish National Collections. As one of his particular interests is the history of costumes, Mr. Mars brings a special flavor of authenticity to his illustrations for *Thanksgiving Day.*